T0104050

THE *Deepest* PART OF ME . . . .

ECHOES OF MY SOUL

TACOMA R. ANDERSON

Order this book online at www.trafford.com
or email orders@trafford.com

Most Trafford titles are also available at major online book retailers.

Print information available on the last page.

ISBN: 978-1-4907-7182-3 (sc)
ISBN: 978-1-4907-7181-6 (e)

Library of Congress Control Number: 2016904696

Trafford rev. 08/19/2017

 Trafford
PUBLISHING® www.trafford.com
North America & international
toll-free: 1 888 232 4444 (USA & Canada)
fax: 812 355 4082

Preface

Thanking God for the gift of Love and the talent in written word. I also thank God for my loving Dad, Hurd F. Anderson, may his legacy of love always live in the generations to follow him, while living taught me to love unconditionally and without fear of rejection. My Son Ahmad who also loves without condition and follows the teachings of Christ. To my church, military and birth families, I love you all.

May God Bless every person who reads these pages of those moments of seeking, wanting and even losing the love, to include the loss of my Dad.

To every person who has touched my life in any capacity, thank you for being an instrument be it positive or negative that has helped me reach a new level at some point in my destiny.

For those who have rejected me, thank you for helping me realize that I am not for everyone and everyone is not for me. For my Spiritual mentors, and there are a lot, I thank God for you planting and watering the seeds of Gods most precious word in my life, that helped me to get beyond the desire for those to love me for my personality but accept me for the Godly Character that God has instilled in me. I thank God for my personal quote for when I sought Him, He showed me where He has brought me: "I found that while running from my destiny, that I gained Character to walk deeper within it"

I hope these pages will help you to heal in the areas that God has healed me and to also bring a growth in your life and help you understand that the Love of God is the deepest part of Me!

Contents

Self Respect

I have found that what my Dad taught me is true
See men are more impressed with the things they
Don't see, verses the ones they do So why,
put all your woman hood on display
Self respect begins with you
When I was younger men didn't want to date me
Why because they told me I was the marrying type
I carried myself in such a way that it was understood
Don't try anything that would disrespect the woman I am
I have come to realize that my inner respect for myself
Is how others feel they must treat me as well
I realized when I didn't respect my body, or myself
Others didn't either
I found that being honest and true to me
Has brought those type of people in my life
I have been friends with people I admire
And they respected me enough to tell me
That they cared for someone else or that we are only friends
See having respect for yourself and others will do the same
For it was out of respect they refused to cause me Pain.
So from my experience please take heed,
No one other than God loves you more than you do yourself
And having respect for yourself sets a
standard that others must adhere
For if they don't they are not your friend

If Only I Could

Many times when we speak I can hear the
hurt, anger and frustration in your voice
It is at those times I wish I had the power to change
all the things that were ever wrong in your life.

Knowing that by changing those things I would
change the essence of the man I have grown to love
If I could I would kiss each pain away the same as I
kissed the bruised skin on our sons arm or leg

If only I could make your life full of the
same joy I feel when I am with you,
Your days would never be without prosperity,
your dreams would all be complete
Your vision would now be a reality and
you would be a satisfied man

If only I could do more for you than pray, and long
to be at your side, If only I could be the oasis of your
strength when you feel faint from the days journey
The weather from which you received
nourishment and growth

If only I could make the changes that
would bring peace in your life
But for now I will be as I have been
in prayer for the man I love
Asking for a renewal of your strength and
peace to rest in your heart and mind
Until the day that your destiny is fulfilled

Can You Phantom

I wonder if you can phantom what it
is for me to feel your caress
To have your hands stroke the curls in my hair
To feel the soft yet strong hands glide
across the curve of my face
Do you even know how much it is for me to feel
your sweet kiss on my lips, on my neck

I wonder if I touch your heart the same as you touch mine,
Each time you ask me the thoughts in my mind
It makes me feel so special to know you
are concerned with my thoughts

I wonder if you know when you touch
me the pleasure it brings
The relief in my heart knowing I am loved sincerely
I wonder if you understand the love I see in your eyes for me
If you know how my body longs to feel
you on, near and in me.....

What Has Become Common

You know it saddens me to see what I
know now has become common
So common that people have lost sight
of the depth of its existence.

It is so common that there is a War where
our military members are dying daily
However it is so common now, that the
news media barely covers it.
Hardly makes mention of it until it hits a record number
Then it is characterized as "This is
the Most Tragic day since"

What is come so common is that fact that OUR
Nation was based on the principals of God, and the
Majority of the people claims to be Christians,
But a Non Believers rights are greater than the
Majority and can demand that all source of Biblical
doctrine be removed from every government place.

It is so common to our cities that Gangs, sell drugs, and
Kill to run what they call their territory and the people
who live there are like prisoners in a foreign land.
Living in fear, and not even trusting of the police who are
suppose to defend them, who they too fear the gangs.
It is too Common that we always want to pass the blame, I
did not know, I was not informed, I was not sure. Is what
we hear even from our top leaders. It is too common that
we don't take responsibility for our on short comings as we
neglect to educate ourselves on the needs of our people

It is too common that we always want someone else to make the first step to take the lead and not want to jump on the wagon until we are sure it is headed for success. Tell me when did our nation turn to cowardness, when our founders and revolutionist made the way of not walking common but Holy ground

Tell me how can we set back and see that a half flown Flag is Common, Do you even stop to think whose life you should be mourning. Is it the dead or those who find this as just common?

The Humanitarian Mission

That is the mission of the human man
The strive to caring and aiding the best he can
The mission of mercy a sign of peace

Oh how quickly can it turn to grief!
All because one groups greed
Many lives lost so uselessly
Yet all you can do is aid in brotherly love and peace
To some human life is as significant as that of a flea
Just wasted without a begging plea
Yes this is a mission
This I do see, but its not only one of a humanitarian
But one to keep sanity
Peace out
Mogadishu Somalia Mass Casualty 9 Jun 1993

Heart of a Soldier

The tensions are rising The missiles light the skies
I pray constantly that we all leave this place alive.
Today my camp received the news
A convoy of my comrades had been ambushed
About twelve are missing No! the word was,
three were killed execution style .The rest are POW's now
We increase on our defenses As now
our mission is increased
Not only to defeat these men but to
get our fallen comrades back
God, Knows we all pray for strength and
a quick end to all this destruction
The news men are here by our side
Sometimes I feel they are in the way
As we continue to fight into another day Rumor
has said that more American's are dead
We are closer to the destination where
we may meet with annihilation
If bio bombs are used each time these
thought run through my mind
I remember this is the life I Chosen so my family
and Friends could continue to be free
I often realize, at moments like this my destiny
has come, a hero I may or may not be
But a soldier I chosen to be fighting
for what my country defends
Sometimes for things I don't believe in Yet, I fight with pride
I have lived a soldier's life with no regret and if need be
I will look death in the eyes and continue to fight
And if for some chance I die
I will die with courage

A Soldiers Thought

I' am here in the place I chose
My life is no longer my own
I do as I am told
I go where my Commander in Chief decides
But so many don't understand
What is placed before my eyes
I see death as it approaches us
I see death as I cause it

Yet, I thank God, I 'm not viewed as a murder
I am only doing my job as a Soldier
My mom, I know she is praying
As we are millions of miles a way
I called her yesterday, just to say
Mom, I love you

I am strong my enemy doesn't see my fear
Only God truly knows how I feel
I know that what I am doing is to protect those I love
It is not an easy thing to do
I am glad I made the choice others were to cowardly to do
I pray that God forgive me for each life I may have to take
I know how their family may feel,,,,
But everyone knows....War is this way!

Mission First------
Taking Care of the Soldier

When you are a new Soldier to the Army
The military world is so strange, so demanding
Yet it is the First Sergeant that makes it feel ok
To be a part of the new way of doing things
It is you the First Sergeant who takes
On the most important Mission
Taking Care of the Soldier
To many they feel that there is nothing more important
Than the organization mission
They are so focused on the goal that the
Resource is often short changed
However, you First Sergeant have always ensured
That the Soldier was taken care of by
Ensuring they were mentally and physically prepared
Encouraging personal and professional growth
Ensuring that the family was ok
Through mentoring, correcting and leading the way
Taking Care of the Soldier often means
Leaving your family to take care of your Military Family
Going to the hospital in the early morning hours
Being there to provide strength in disarray
Being the disciplinarian when a Soldier strays
Yet, through the years, you provided consistent Care
Through the unselfish sacrifices of time you committed
To ensure that a Soldier stays within Army Standards
Soldier excels beyond their own expectations
Teaching future Leaders Guiding in
time of War as well as Peace
You are the perfect example of what it is to honestly
Take Care of Soldiers

Missing You

The precious little moments how they
seem to leave us all alone
The time we spend together enhances
our love, and causes our desires
to flow like a raging flood
Now, I am here in a world where you
love to fight and fight for blood
The times I have alone I long for your
love, your touch, and your kiss
Just knowing you care helps me go one day by day
I think and long for the day when we can
be together again side by side
Until the day we die. I love you with my
heart, my body and my soul
Because you are the love of my life with a heart made of gold
I want "US" to be together to grow old with you
I love you

Needing You

Life 's games are so unkind
People hurt others and think nothing of it
Why do things happen and the innocent are framed
While the guilty run free

Why do people always try to destroy the love we share
This love between you and me
Its at times like this I want to cry
I just don't know how people could be so unkind
Unfeeling and so cruel. I just want to be there
with you and hold you in my arms to
make all my hurt go away!!

Sirens in my Ear

Today as every day since we met when I hear sirens I
think of you. I think of your dedication to humanity
as you take on the call of duty with your
Fellow firefighters or paramedics to rescues people as
simple as me who Have encountered a sudden impasse in
life where they are now dependant on your skills to save
them. You train so hard so vigorously to ensure that you
Are able to carry someone out the burning flames or
that you can actually use the Jaws of Life to Free them
from what use to be a car, now just a crumbled
Piece of material that has trapped them helplessly
within I think about what could possibly run
through your mind when you hear those alarms
ring in the middle of the night as you and your
comrades hurry to make it to the destination
Not certain what you will find, not knowing if
someone is hurt Not knowing if you will have to free
them I wonder if you say a quick prayer and ask for
God's strength and his guidance to bring you all out
safely from the danger you are Headed to tame
I wonder what goes through your mind as a family stands
by on the Banks of the water, as you search for their son or
daughter as they hope for a rescue from a possible drowning
and as time has passed it turns to a recovery mission instead
I think of all these things you face each day, The joys
of life, the pain of lost, the sorrow of Love ones gone.
I think of the unthinkable sights your eyes may see
and then I understand the beauty of who you are
how you have learned to balance these moments The
good and the bad, and just enjoy life in simplicity.

Echo's of the Past

NO, my brother, I apologize I don't get excited
about black history month As most do
Why should I celebrate my heritage for 28 days? 29 if the
year decides to leap No, Don't hate, I m not a creep
I choose to celebrate my black heritage Each and everyday
I respect my black hero's who paved the way
by leading marches without violence....You
do remember Martin Luther King Jr
But when you celebrate do you remember
The Rosa Parks, the Harriet Tuggmans, the Malcolm X's
Who also fought for change
When you choose to sing...D o you remember The
Mahalia Jackson's, Etta James, and Sarah Vaughn's
I celebrate my creativity each time I write a poem
As I long to be as Great as Langston
Hughes and Maya Angelo
But, when I listen to the new rhythm
and blues and Hip Hop
I think about the Count Basie's, Duke
Ellington's, and Cab Callaway's Oh yeah, let's
not forget the tribute to Miles Davis as
They changed the music style in their day. I notice how
we often reflect on just a few of our wonderful leaders
Of the past. Those who became the first Like Jackie
Robinsons, Arthur Ashes, and now the Williams sisters.
So, my questions to you my friend in why wait to
February To begin to learn of our Marcus Garveys,
Josephine Bakers, and Marion Anderson's
If any a name I have mentioned you do not know I
challenge you, my sister, and my brother to research

Their contribution to our black revolution Learn
about the horrible plights, the Tuskegee Airmen,
The Buffalo's and now our Colleen Powell's

Look at how we have Trusted God And surpassed what
others wanted us to achieve I was challenged to do just
this Explain why 28 days is not enough for me To learn
and comprehend what others Have endured for me to have
the things I often take for granted But remember where
you came from is the Down the path others have beaten
And expects for you to carry out and raise a standard
To never be ignorant,
never be unequal,
and never forget....
These rights
This freedom
Wasn't Free!

Just say Yes

From the moment I first laid eyes on you I said Yes, he is .....
So many different things ran through the canvas of my mind
I just had to find out who you were,
to learn your style to know
What causes you to do the things you do

I saw a man, but not just any man a Renaissance man
A man who is about change, finding a new adventure,
Living life on the edge, yet remaining true to the very
Being that God had created

A man with no fear, strong with passion filled with intensity
All I could do is from the inside out hear loudly
The song by Floetry, just say YES
It was with so much of me I wanted to say yes to you ...
Yet I stood quietly listening to you express your thoughts
Your dreams your desires for your life
I could only say yes, those are similar to mine
Yes, It could be so much that we do have in common
Then when I thought your focus was on someone else
You let me know not so, and in my mind I screamed
Yes
I just wanted to know if I could have caught your attention
The way you caught mine and as we spoke
time seemed not to pass and the endless
Things that we shared views, desires, ideas, goals
And in my heart I smiled, and sighed yes
I will have a friend, and who knows more
But all I can say for now is Yes, I want to see more.

The Best in me

God how is it that you see the Best in me.
The soul who has been cleansed with
the Blood of your Son Jesus,
The child who is now pure and transparent to your eyes.

God how is it that you see the very best in me,
The one you have called out of the darkness
The one you have saved from Sin, sexual desire
The one you keep from being murdered, from suicide
The one you delivered from abuse, neglect, strive and envy
You see me as one you have Chosen to do your work
And yet those who are also your children
whom you have done the same for
whose sin you removed choose to see the very worst in me.
How is it that you have done the same for them yet,
It seems impossible for you to have
cleansed me and deliver my soul
God how is it possible for you to see the Best in me
and your Children still try to deny
what you have done for me?

Pride for My Stride

You say you like my walk, yet you call me conceded
You see how I hold my head high
Yet to you I am sidity
I find it such a pity that your views of me are so SH***

Yet, if you know of the mountains I have crossed
I have earned the right to hold my head high
If you only know of the low points from which I have risen
You would just begin to comprehend the Pride I have

For the women you see is one who
will overcome anything.....
For I have!
I can archive all that I set out to do
for I am not limited like you
I trust in God!
I believe "ask and it shall be given"
So don't resent me! Especially for the woman I chose to be
Admit your admirations and strive to be a seeker of
Wisdom and knowledge just as me!
So smile! As I walk by with my head held high

The Ultimate Quest of Life

How can I begin to understand your journey
to the Ultimate Quest of Life?
The longing to have the relationship with God that
Adam shared before he sinned in the Garden of Eden.
How can I possibly began to understand the
desired to walk with God as Adam Did in the
cool of the day, sharing his love his vision
How can I understand the longing, the yearning the
unfulfilled hunger that you have To regain that lost
connection to God that sin caused with Adam.
How can I possibly know what it is to have that
relationship where only God knows me, my
heart, my dreams, my visions, my feelings of
incompleteness, unworthiness, impurity
How can I possibly know what it is to seek God's face
and still feeling as if I am not satisfying his call,
How can I possibly know what it is to hear the
voice of God and run from it instead of to it
How can I possibly know what it is to finally answer
God's call and still slip away into a backslidden state.
How can I possibly understand the decision to be totally
Sold out to God, tarry before his throne in prayer, seeking
to have the dark voids filled with his light his love,
How can I possibly begin to understand the
struggle of the flesh, the desire of the opposite
sex, to be next to me, and still long to be in the
Kingdom Business, and resist the temptation.
How can I truly understand the feeling of being alone
on the journey for the Ultimate love, the Ultimate
end and still feel as if I will never make it there,

How can I ever know what it is to be on the
Quest of my life, mortal and immortal Knowing
that Only God can bring me there
Tell me how can I relate to how you feel, If I was
not walking on that path to the Quest of my soul
Salvation, and heeding the Call of God?
How could I possibly begin to understand?

Through Loving Eyes

I wish that you could see yourself through my eyes
For the vision is not blinded nor is it tainted
I wish you could understand and accept
my desire to be near you
And long to have you as part of my
world, an extension to me
The man I see is one who Loves God
with every ounce of his being
Your Passion is so strong to heed the
Call of God on your life
At times I see you as you fight the mental battle
The emotional battle of feeling that you will never achieve

The Vision God has birthed in your spirit
The Vision that has become the very Essence of You
Through my eyes you would see yourself as you are in
the mist of your storms holding even
tighter to the hands of God
Resting assured that your Soul is Anchored
in his Love and his Word
I see you seeking to always be before the Throne of God
Not for your own reasons, but to seek the
Strength, Wisdom and Knowledge for
others whose path you will cross
Those who don't know God as closely as you but desires too

I see you Ministering, Leading, Teaching, Pastoring
To those who no longer want to be where they are in life
I see you pulling on the Pain of your past
As you use it to ignite the Passion in your Heart to
Never be Lost, or without God ever again

I see you as a Man, who a woman should
Love, Cherish and Encourage as you not only take
Your Stand for God, but most importantly as you Walk
In his Kingdom, carrying out his Will and Calling

I Understand your position in life
I find myself as an Intercessor, a Prayer Warrior
And if allowed an Armor Bearer for you
As you walk down the Path of your
Spiritual Calling from God

For my eyes see you with the love
my heart has grown to feel
and my mind can no longer deny
If only you could see me as I do you
Through Loving Eyes

Simple Complexity

he simple things that are the most intimate part of a being,
Meets the ever complex moments in time,
that guides us through life
And every now and then,
there is a smile, a hello, a glance, so simple
that it intrigues you to seek out the complexity,
for nothing can be just as it seems
for the smile is always welcoming me,
inviting me so to speak, come to my world
chat with me,
learn of the things that you see are
the mysteries behind my eyes
that seems to smile when I glance upon you.
Just the simple moment that entered
to the deeper realm of knowing, understanding
More of the complexities that are
truly what I see as simplicity
but only someone like you could see...
.because you sought for that complexity
that is truly simplicity

Voice in the Mirror

I look in the mirror and I pray to God that just
as Jabez, that I cause no one any pain
Even though my choices in life have
not brought me the same
I hear the voice in my mirror as I see the reflection of me
I hear it as it seems to scream out to me. Let me be Free!
Free me from this place you have
trapped me – Let me be Free!
Release me from the horrible things
in your past... Let me be Free!

Let me be the substance that is now your strength
Release me from those you find as your enemy
Let go of this hurt you allowed others to dump on your life
Embrace me as the very air your breathe

Don't let bitterness reside any longer within
as it is cutting off the very life in me
Set me free from the only eyes that are yours to see. Let
me be free to show the inner beauty locked deep within

Let me speak of the trails, the tribulations,
the deliverance of God
Set me free in the world outside that is cold that
as others look upon you look upon me
Reflect upon your beauty locked so deeply away,
trapped beyond the pupils of your eyes

The passion that makes the heart beat loud---the pounding
of the echoes of me screaming loud ....Set me Free
As God has you to share the deliverance from the Pain

Release the Hurt-
Release the shame,
let the thing I see as you look upon me ....
Set me free to go to the places that only air can flow
Let others feel what I only see each
time your reflect upon me

Set me free,
let me do what God has Called you to do
Allow me I beg you
Set me free .....
Free to Love

Whisper

Sometimes I ponder on how you entered my world,
I know the glance we shared but I guessed ...
Did you hear the whisper of my heart
telling you I was seeking Love
Was the whisper of my heart so loud that
it was like a scream in your ear?
Did the whisper come from the look in my eyes
as you seen into the depth of my soul?
I am not sure if you even heard the whisper
I thought I heard you whisper to me
I want to know who you are
When you hugged me so unexpectedly and quickly
As you appeared you were gone
I wandered did you hear the whisper of my hands as I
Embraced you when you hugged me,
And slide it down you arm as you walked away?
A sweet whisper of a loving heart
lead to the tender whisper of a massaging hands.
That lead to the sensual whisper of the
succulent taste of the sweetest lips
that lead to the whisper
Good night.

Awakening

It was so subtle, as the sun rising over the horizon
Warming the earth with its gentle rays reaching out
Over the sea and once darkened land

That is how those precious few
but valuable moments with you were like
I found myself basking in the rays of
your confidence and Assured ways
I soaked up each touch of your hand as it held mine
Or guided me in a new direction

For once in an unexpected moment
I allowed my control to be overtaken
But not in an overpowering way

The Love inside my heart, The desires I locked away in
a suppressed and secure place
deep in my soul and mind.
The desire I was sure had faded, if not died
It began to awaken

I began to desire your touch
I was as eager as the desert is for rain
To hear your voice speak anything
But especially to me

I found myself beginning to open up
Like the petals of a blossoming flower or
Even more when I was with you
I had become that butterfly breaking free
From the dark place I had ran too
Waiting for the warmth and moment to break free
To spread my wings and fly into
Loving arms that awakened the once
Dying Love in Me.

Life Continues to Move

My tears are now like the rain falling so softly,
quietly down my face
Each time I cry over what I desired it is as if God
Allows the rain to fall to mask the tears
Eventually, I will learn
As I thought I had,
But yet this is the hardest lesson, the test for me to pass
When I bear my heart's desire
even more the inner part of my soul
while other seem to see that as
unwanted, unsolicited and undesired
I find myself asking
How did I get those signals wrong
Life continues to move.....

Something to hold

In my youth I wanted someone to hold on too
Someone who was cut, his body well defined
His muscles were like a washboard
Then I wanted more physical than now The
something to hold on to was the physical ...
Yet I was left longing
I was once married the thing I longed to hold on to Was
the vows I made to God and the man I had chose
The one thing I desired was the love we professed I
was amidst, for it was no truth there on his part
Only on mine, and then still I was
left longing for something
Something, not someone to hold on to
Now that I am single, I know the desire for the physical
I know the touch of the man; I know the stroke of his
Touch, I know the deceit in his heart, I know the truth
In his soul, I know not all is like my past, I am sure, for
I know, that the one that I need to hold on too
Is God
I still long for the one man to hold
on too, not for the physical
Yet the mental intimacy, that becomes the spiritual intimacy
That thing that was so deep that
nothing but God could fulfill
Only the one he was to bring could
satisfy those moments of desire
That could touch the heart, the mind and depth of my soul
The one who would teach me, pray with me
The one that would want to hold on to me
And I would have not only something
but someone to hold on too

Sweet Moments in Time

There you were lying cozy in my bed
Sheets caressing you
as I often desire when I am away from you
Sleeping in such a peaceful state
With a slight smile on your face
I stood there and looked
As several thoughts passed through my mind
Of what could be
I just stood there admiring the wonderful essence
That you exude
Knowing that I was forever changed
From our first encounter
Knowing that I had once given up on finding
Peace in my heart or trusting in one person
All that changed when our eyes met and I felt
The gentle touch of your strong hands
guide me to our table to eat
The conversation had me so captivated that I
blocked out everything that surrounded us
I focused only on what you had to share
Knowing that I could only learn
Now as time has pasted
You are here next to me
And all I desire is to lay here
Next to you and enjoy these sweet moments in time
Until they continue to be no more

You and I

The day we met was the happiest day of my life
For it was on that day I found you My Love!!
From that moment on I could see my life in its fulfilled state
Every since that day I have experienced
an undying love for you
I would do anything to make you happy
even if it meant letting you go
Just because I love you that much
To me, you are my moonlight on the darkest night
My sunshine in the rain and my
comfort when I have been hurt
or just experiencing pain
No one else can ever love me the way that you do !!
Because you are the love of my life and I would die for you
Just as you would for me
I thought you needed to know that I love you
I will always be there for you
I love you because you are a special part of my life
One that I could never let completely let go
I pray I never have to either
I love you my love

Love almost as deep...

From the moment we first shared words, the moments
we shared by the water, to the moments in my mind
now your words, your scent and your smile
I have yet to release from my thoughts I can remember
this from you The sincerity in your eyes, Yet I seen
pain, and non-trust, I seen hope, and strength.
These words made me yearn to know
and share with you more
"I finally found someone whose love
is almost as deep as mine..."
I have yet to find a man who could respect or handle
the love I have to give to know that someone could
love deeper than me made me want to know it
I just wanted to feel a drop of the love
like a raindrop on my face
Such a warm gentle refreshing thing, to feel the rain,
Or a morsel of your affection
The time flew and off you went as quick as you came
I thought of Haley's comet for a moment
For it seems that I encountered a man, like that comet
For most a once in a life time event,
Yet what good is an encounter if you are not ready
For the beauty of the moment, I mean,
I have close the door to the thought of love
and having one of my own but for a brief moment,
I looked in the eyes of a man
Who thought his love was deeper than mine
Yet, our hearts left unchanged, just touched

Would You Let Me…..?

Let me touch the depth of you
Allow me to go where others only desire
Let me get next to the heat of your fire
The warmth of your heart

Let me caress your body
Make love to your mind
Others only want your body
I want you! the truth of you

Allow me to be your heart's desire
To know your pain
To enjoy your love

Making love to the body is great
Yet making love to the heart and mind
Is Ecstasy that only a select few ever find

For me, I prefer to love deeper than the physical
So deep it is only known as spiritual
Feel me completely as I love you deeper
than any other can or will

Will you let me?

Beyond a Moment

I am here alone wanting you to call
Wanting to feel your touch
Wanting to be engulfed with the passions of my love for you

As the rain falls down from the sky
I want it to be the be the rhythm of you between my thighs
Gentle tears I seem to cry as alone
in my bed I continue to lay

Longing to feel your body lying next to mine
So hard to have such a wonderful affair
with someone who doesn't know just how much you care

Or know you even long to have them near,
but love is the melody of your voice,
the comfort of your smile. And all the while I am here
longing to feel him ever so close to me
I understand all you have to give, all you have to share
But do you truly know deep inside how much I care

Do you understand to what extent I want to share with you?
Each and every part of me, all of the
truth within, to unleash
My passion without restraint to touch every part of you

Your heart, mind, body, and depth of your soul. I want to
Fulfill your desire and never let you
go, Beyond a moment in life
Alone ever again, Searching for the love I have to give

Deposit

I wonder what it is that you took from
your time spent with me
What morsel of my being did you take
to satisfy the hunger in your soul
What part of your time spent with me will you never let go
Tell me, for I question what it is

Was it the passion of each of my touches, my kisses?
Was it the passion in the intellect as we spoke?
Was it the passion in the words I write
inspired by the feelings, I hold for you
Was it the passion of the way I live life
Was it the passion of the dreams you
seen me turn into my reality
Was it the passion of the drive that
helped me to achieve my goals?
Was it the passion in my role as a mother, a
disciplinarian and sometimes father?

I wonder if it was even the passion that is within me
I wonder if it was my mere character
I wonder if it is my morals, my values, my trust
I wonder if you understood the value
of the friendship I displayed
I wonder if you understood, why, or if you even cared
Now that you are not in my mist, I wonder
Do you even reflect as I have to think of what it is?
The deposit you left behind in my heart my mind
Or was it just as any other passing phase in your life
Was I like the sun going down and a
passing of the average day?
Or was I like that significant event that will
always forever in your heart remain

Dark Temptation

The scent of you Dark Temptation seemed to
Grasp me by my pheromones, and hypnotized me
It was a sweet seduction of my senses as if it
Were your voice, whispering the things I desired so much
And your hands gentle caress as you made love to my mind
with the thoughts of your strong and
youthful body taking over mine

Such soft succulent lips, which made
me, carve the taste of them
Because of the words spoken so sincerely
So many of my unspoken desires did you divulge
as if you have always been a part of me

A dark sweet temptation greater than
The finest chocolate I've ever tasted
So bold and confident in your flavor
In your taste, it is truly your strength
How you have to offer so much to the unexpecting
And the so desiring
Sweet seductive Dark temptation making
One wavier on the thoughts of self indulgence
of such a great delicacy

Broken Promise

Do you cherish my love and every moment we have together?
Do you pray that we are always in love with one another?
Are you happy with this love we share?

Promises and things planned never to come to pass
The things I believed
Now I feel like a fool
How could you promise all those things
and never go through with them?
Don't you realize ?
Can't you see just have much I love you ?
I love you so much it hurts
Like a thorn of a rose
How can something so beautiful cause so much pain?

It Hurt Me to the Core

It hurt me to the core of my very being,
The pain was worse than ripping my heart right out of me
You, the man I love the one I trusted, the one
I invested all my time, all these years
It hurt me to the core of my mere existence, this pain
I don't understand why or how you felt I need not know
About the child you had, yet you robed me of that dream
The joy of being a mother having one of my own
As you told me we were enough for one another,
How can you be so casual so nonchalant about this situation
As if it was a mere payment on a loan you had
This is a child, even though not mine, a part of you
You took away my choice, to accept to be angry,
All you left me with it pain, and betrayal
Yes, it hurt me to the core,
My body is in total shock; my heart no longer desires to beat
Everything I knew as truth is all tainted with lies
I wonder, how you felt, each time you seen a child
Knowing you had one, knowing you denied me of one
How could you be so bold as to lie
to me over and over again?
Did you enjoy the pain it brought me?
Did you think it would make me want you still?
Did you realize I was not as weak as you had determined
For today, I told you I desire you no more,
Today, I saw my lawyer, I no longer will be hurt to my core,
By the one that I once adored
The healing begins, from the inside out, the core of me
Is not rotten by the lies, and deceit you brought in
It is rejuvenated by the love I hold in me
Know me, loving me. So I refuse to hurt
anymore, especially in my core.

Blue Phoenix Rising

Through the storms and struggles of
life, the Blue Phoenix has risen
Even when abandoned by those who should have loved
She rose above the rejection
Even through the abuse of family
through their words and actions
Yet she rose to the higher calling
The passion inside her was ignited her desire
to live to love it drove her to rise
Focused on the what is to be instead of what was not,
Blue Phoenix found herself reaching out to Love,
The only love she has ever known,....God
It was in God that she
found her place, her strength, and understanding
It is only on the promises of God that she could stand
Blue Phoenix rose above all that was
to destroy her only because
The one who loves and directs her path was greater
Than anything that could destroy her
And it is her faith in God that continues to allow the
Rise of the Blue Phoenix
Whose flame is blue for it is the strongest and hottest
Part of her passion to live and love

NO Work - No Pay

You look at me as if I had no feeling for my child
Yet the picture you see is not complete
The frustration of my tone is that of a single parent home
No work means No Pay

As a child sick at home to stay
The doctor's booked, hours I must wait
Yet how can I give him more when
NO work means No Pay

But to you as you look to me sees a parent upset
Who has no compassion
How wrong you are my friend
For what you see is a matter of twisted of a single mother's
Journey when the child support is delayed
When the rend and insurance is due
How is e going to get fed
When No work mean No Pay
So don't look at me with such dismay
When what you see is a shallow part
of reality of a single parent
And their deeper concerns
When No Work Means No Pay

Fire and Ice

I am one called Fire and Ice....
for I have learned to live in balance
that my power lies not in the essence of my beauty
it is within the power of my thoughts
which controls my actions.
I understand that love and Anger are the fire and Ice,
even thought I can love to the extreme,
It will always stay balanced but the
Anger is a different flame
that can melt the Ice and turn it to water that
will eventually destroy the total being. ....
therefore I am the rose of Fire and Ice,
my thorns are not ones that cause pain to others
just simple reminders of the battle that now lies behind me
that I used once to climb higher
as I began to bloom into the sweet
essence of the woman I am today,
one that understands that the outer petals
last only for the season of the spring,
then I must remove the layers of the pain,
the stress, and only allow the inner
beauty to radiate outward
to draw the person to the core of my being
this is where the sweet nectars of the love is.....

Man in my Dreams

I close my eyes to rest each night
And in my dreams we meet
Each moment is a timeless event
Where I at last am secure

I found myself showing my weakness
And removing my guard
And regardless of what you see
You always seem to remain intrigued

When things seem to get me down
It is in your voice I find peace
And reassure is always there

I had once leaded myself to believe that...
I could only have these moments in my dreams.
Now I share them with you
Each time you call,
each time you write
every time you smile
and always when we touch

Lady In Waiting

I will be to you alone a lady in waiting
for you my man to return home

I am a virtuous women......
One who is above all measure
And for you alone
Shall know the depth of my inner most pleasure

I am here for you......
Waiting in solemn, anticipating those
Delicate, seductive touches
The tender embraces of your lips
The security of your arms wrapped around me

Longing to be engulfed with your passions and your song
Yet, until then.......
Just know that I am here....
For your alone, your lady in waiting
Love sincerely me

The Search

To many people life is a never ending game
To some it is just living from day to day
Living in a world full of dreams and struggles
But out there somewhere
There is a person living like me!
Searching through their life looking for love
Soon I know their life will be filled
They will find their love and for them Life will be complete
But until then they will just be searching in their life...

Moments Gone

I Sit here thinking of the minutes in our past
Now you are my husband, finally at last
Our romance was long,
Our passion not gone
We sit here all alone
Just thinking of moments gone
We built our lives
We made them strong
While sitting here in our brand new home
Just remembering those moments gone
When we look into each other's eyes
We remember the days gone by.....
Our struggles and our triumphs
We will always cherish
For were able to remember
The days and moments gone by

Beneath the surface of my eyes

How can a total stranger view into my eyes
And see the things the one I love can not
How can they reach inside me and
know the deepest Thought
As if my soul were screaming out to them
Without even being in my mist

How can a total stranger know how I long to have that one
The one who will love me and hold my heart in his hands
As if he were protecting a baby dove
The one who would know the pain, yet never cause it
The one who would share his time and his affection
The one who would never leave me longing

I was so surprised, so intrigued and so vulnerable
How could I be such an open book to someone looking in
Yet, the one closest to me, the one I long to have
The one next to me, does not desire to see or know
The truth that lies beneath the surface of my eyes

Which should I Choose?

Which one should I chose because I am
So enticed by them both,
One sings the Rhythm and blues
His tune is so sweet that it soothes
The lonely thoughts and feelings that enter my mind

The other strokes the bass of his guitar
To make it speak words of deep passion to me
Reminds me of the moments I so long to share
Having him run his fingers through my hair
Slow sensual massages from the mind to the toe

Deep inside I still don't know which one I should chose
For both of them touch me in a different way
They are both able to penetrate beyond the walls I have built
To protect my heart from the pain I once felt,

It is the sweetest sound I hear the song, the melody
The honesty in each note
But it is the truth in the vibe the movement that his
Bass brings to my body as he puts voice in his strings
Which should I pursue or should I say which has chosen me

For the song bird continually sings,
but the bass is something
I experience only when the moon seems to be full
Reminding me of the love my heart longs to enjoy

Dangerous Chemistry

It was my walk that caught your eye,
The chemistry in the sway of my hips, my thighs
Then you glimpse into the depth of my eyes
To your surprise it was Chemistry from the start
To many searching they would never know
The depths of my mind the echoes of my soul
Yet you stroked my passion open my heart and
Massaged my mind
Though intense conversation from the serious
To the hilarious, you accepted me
As I had accepted you
The chemistry was so honest
So free, just as the bass of your guitar,
Making my heart pound with excitement
As time passed us by the world seemed to stand still
The realness of the possibility to gain so much
That others have let slip by the possibility of the
Things that lay within the reach of our grasp
The Dangerous chemistry that was in the kiss
the kiss that made you want to through all
caution to the wind and take passion by its
hand and release all that was within the thoughts
that each touch caused us to feel.
This mad dangerous chemistry
I would have never known If I didn't
Chose to release the number to my phone.
It was neither

How could I allow myself to read the vibes so wrong?
For it was neither of the two
It was not the song bird that sings so sweet
So softly and yet so loud and strong
Hoping his one true love would hear his song
Across the hundreds of country mile that stands
Between them now not really their choice but their destiny
That is the reason his melody is so sweet to me
I understand his longing to be with the one who is not near

It was not the bass player that made his strings speak words
To the depth of my soul for he is so consumed
He only noticed me for a moment when he
Let his eyes wonder over the horizons plain
Only to find me as that quick distraction
For that brief enticing attraction

The stimulated mind, quick moments in time only
Lead to the subliminal communicated
thoughts as I misinterpreted
The voices in their eyes, the longing to be with one who
Could fulfill the echoes of their soul

NO need to knock, they will go unanswered

I finally got the nerve to tell him
To tell him, I cared, that I wanted to
be the woman in his life
When I asked what he would do if another
woman walked into his life
Not mentioning me, eluding to me
He said, I would not let it happen, no one can come in
I asked the question for a second time
And the responds was the same,
See I am here, in his world, unknown to him
I am a dear friend, and yet to him, he is blind
To blind to see that I compliment all that is him

We sit and talk for hours on end, I am frequently at his side
Yet, in his eyes, I can only be a close friend
I find love to be a funny,

And even cruel thing to place a wonderful person in my life
One that encompasses all that I prayed for in my mate
One who is not self consumed, but
loving and true to all he loves
But he would never allow my knocks on
his hearts door to be answered

I am on the other side of the wall,
Knowing, hearing, understanding his frustrations,
Sharing his joys, successes, as he does mine
Longing for his laughter to continue in my presence,
All the while knowing he will never answer my knocks
For he has made it clear, he would never allow anyone
Other than the one he has always loved

Eclipse of Love

So often love will present itself ready and available
And we as humans, as beings driven by our personal
Gains, our careers begin to eclipse the
possibility to allow it to grow

Love can present itself in the man who seems so wrong
Only to the family of the one receiving the love
For he has too many tattoos, or body
piercing, he is so wrong
Others opinions begin to eclipse the love that is there
For his outer person has nothing to do with his heart

Love can present itself a ready able being,
Yet family and friends once again will eclipse the possibility
Because see his is not the right race, class, or education
Yet that has nothing to do with the love
and passion he has to offer

So often we will eclipse love, with the pain of our past
We fail to embrace it for what it is,
Yet we eclipse it with comparison of what
others have told us it should be

The heart longs, to know the warm passions of love, and
To carry out the desire that comes as its companion
If only we will allow it to be full as
the moon on the clear night
Not cloud it with past experience, others view,
If we would only accept it embrace it
and stop eclipsing the Love

Kindred Spirit…..Sacred Heart

Two souls walking, seeking to reach the promise of God
One sought their rib, the other waited for Boaz
Both loved God with all the essence of
their spirit, soul, and human mind
For they both sought God for wisdom,

As time passed with various trials,
tribulations and circumstance
The failed romances, and the battered hearts,
Scorn and broken heartedness drew them closer to God

Still seeking to overcome the constant
healing wounds of the past
Two kindred spirits grow in wisdom,
and knowledge of God's word
Learning the joy found in the Sacred heart
of God and his love for his child

The two traveling different paths, met at the cross roads
And because they could agree, because
their journey was one of solace
They joined their hearts, their minds
to keep one another up lifted
And walked unto the next level of their destiny
As they sought to find the depth of God's most sacred heart.

Earth is mourning

The clouds are gloomy as if the earth needs to cry
A moment of sadness
You may question why?
The earth is mourning as more of our soldiers die

Mothers, wives, and daughters wonder why
My son, my lover, my daddy had to die
Why did he have to get killed this way?
Why did they ask for help in saving someone?
And then take advantage of his humanity
And take his life

God I know it was just his time
But, I wanted to talk to him, hold him
Just one more time

The greatest lesson I have ever learned
Never forget to express my love
For no minute pass now is ever promised

He died as hero, at least in my eyes
He was moving in a peaceful manner
When death took him over
I thank God; I had the chance to know him
His smile, his touch
His wisdom and his love
But for now it is a time for mourning

In your Memory MOM

I am glad that God blessed me to be your daughter
To have you hold my hand and keep me
from Hurting myself when I was small

To have you teach me how to comb my hair Shop
for clothes and the value of my individuality
I am blessed to have you Mom to teach me
That my beauty lies within my heart not in the things I wear

I have been blessed to have you as my Mom
To encourage me as my life took challenging turns
When my heart was first broken, it was your love
Your smile, that let me know I could go on

I was blessed with you Mom, as you taught me How
to fight with all the strength I have within me
As I watched you and supported your battle with cancer
I love you for never giving up.

I was blessed to be here today, by your side, as you
Took the hand of God and joined him in heaven
I know you love me, as I love and treasure you
I don't see this as good bye, but I will see you soon.
I love you and miss you more than you will know

Thank you Mom for always being a woman to admire,
For being a woman people grew to love
For being a woman of strength, for sharing your love
And teaching me to be the strong wife, and mother as you
I love you.
Love me.

Memorable moments with You- Dad
(Mr. England from his son)
As time has passed from my birth to the present day
You have always been the one to share
your warmth, knowledge and love
It was you who taught me how to walk,
talk and respect my elders

It was you Daddy that taught me how
to treat women as Queens
And which women were not for me,
as you tossed me the keys
To the car that you first allowed me to
drive even when I had no permit
I will always remember the way you
would say "Hey, young man"
As I walked through the door after being away at college
It was your wisdom that helped me through the rough times,
Through the women troubles, through the divorce

It was that same great wisdom that helps me
as I pass it on to my own children
I will always hold fast to the days
when we would sat and talk
How you would tell me things that would
help guide me through life
I remember how you stood in the door
as I would go out in the world
Discovering new challenges, seeking new adventures
I recall the pride in your voice as you say I love you

I love the fact that you sharing your love, your thoughts,
your weaknesses, as well as your strengths, your fears,
you taught me that a real man has these qualities
I love how you faced the worst in life,
and kept God in first place

These and other things I will always remember
About you as you lived and even as I have to say today
See you later, as you are gone to live a better life.
I will never regret, the times we shared,
I am glad I told you each day I could, I love you Dad.

A Call that was not unanswered

I called you today Dad to tell you how much
I care how much I love you
For the first time, in my life you didn't answer me

I know that you got the call I so dreaded you to get
See, I am selfish when it comes to you Dad,
I share you only because I have to,
I want each minute of your time you have to give

Over the years, it has been your wisdom that has guided me
You have taken my friends in and loved them like me
Never, have I called on you and you were not there for me

I have so much to be so grateful for, as God allowed me to
Share so many fond memories.
So, Dad, know I understand you got
the invitation you so longed
To receive, the invitation to life in eternity.
I read the poems you left for us to
read give me the reassurance
That you are ok. Dad, I am glad you answered God's Call

Even though I long to have you here because I am selfish,
I would rather have you there with God,
So rest in his glory, know my love is great
for you but Gods is Greater

In Loving Memory of Shante Wells

A brief span of life and a miracle you did see
Even though you never heard Shante speak aloud
The words Mommy, Daddy or I love you too.
Each glance upon your face she did see
And each smile she returned reassured you
Your little miracle did think....
That's my mommy and daddy, I love you too.
Though the years were short here for Shante on earth
They were greater than what man predicted at her birth

Shante is now deeper in your heart,
much deeper than ever before
I know you will miss her cry, her laugh and smile
When you go about your days
Trust and know your miracle will be
with you every moment in your heart

Though Shante has left this body behind her on earth
She smiles and laughs in Heaven,
Where with God we know she lives
Until the day we make it there too
We reflect on the blessing of her life
We can smile in our hearts for we know a part of Shante
Is always a thought a way each time we think of
Heaven's newest Angel Shante

The Beauty of Iris Kenny

When you look upon the Iris flower you
see God's hand out reached in love
You see His wisdom in its beauty as
it takes in the rays of sun
It brings joy to the heart of one who is
blessed to receive the hearts gift
It is one to be admired, cherished and is as delicate
as its courage and the faith it took helped it grow
When looking in the eyes of Deaconess Iris
Kenny, her love was always on display, as the vast
array of the flower whose name she shared
Her laughter and conversation would win over
any soul and enhance all who was blessed to
hear her story, her journey and her strength
There was never a moment that fear took hold for she
had Faith that God guided her each place she would go
God extended his hand and picked this precious
flower to enter into his eternal bouquet of souls
We rejoice in God's decision as Iris took
her place in God's kingdom
as we mourn in our loss no one can deny the impact
her life made on those God used her to touch
For her love was as gentle, subtle and as beautiful
as the delicate flower she was named
I am blessed and forever grateful I shared a
moment of time in worship and friendship
with Iris my beautiful sister in God.

In Loving Memory of my beautiful friend Iris Kenny.

Rivers of Stone

I went to visit with you today
I was there in the rivers of stones,
I sat on the bench by the water fountain,
I looked at the tulips by the wall

Others see it as monuments,
I know what is truly there
I see the souls of many like you Dad
Those who sacrificed their life
Those who gave it all,
Some for their country others for their family
Others for their battle buddy.

I know you are comfortable resting in the arms of God
But still as I sat here next to your grave
I still long to feel your arms wrap around me
For in your love to me you gave me your all
I love and miss your wisdom that has
guided me through the years

But I know you are at rest deep in the Arms of God
And from time to time I will come here
To the rivers of stone to pay my respect and gratitude
To not only you because of my love for you
But to those like you who gave it all

My Angel Danielle's Return Home

My angel Danielle, your name means "God is my Judge"
It was taken from the bible, from Daniel
God was his Judge and deliver from the lion's den
My lovely Angel he delivered you from
the clutches of death at birth

You were a blessing and a miracle from the start
The doctors had declared you dead, I prayed to God
Breathe life into my child, I promised to love you regardless
God did answer my prayers, He
touched your lungs, and voice
He allowed you to cry loud enough for someone to hear you

Many nights, I sat next to you watching
you grow, thanking God
For each breath you took. He blessed
me with an angel he selected
Just for me, and trusted me with the
ability to love and care for you

It never mattered to me your eyes never
saw my face, your ears never
Heard my voice, your lips never spoke my
name. Each time you hugged me
Each time you cuddled me, I knew your
love, and it was always in your smile
And those big brown eyes of yours. I
watched the past 18 years pass by
Thanking God each day you lived, and
for each moment I have you near

My greatest gift was your life, my greatest joy
was teaching you, sharing with you
But most of all loving you for the miracle
child you were and became to me

I knew the day you were born I would
have you for a short time
I thank God for he blessed our family
with his angel for these 18 years
Our family has experienced the unconditional
love, and trust that God has
Given us, each time you smiled, you
laughed, you touched us all

On today, God called you his angel home.
Our hearts is sadden but our lives are
blessed with the treasured memories
Of the moments you shared. The love
for you doesn't stop here
Until we meet in heavens courts I pray
our love transcends time
And death that you always feel our love for you

A Century of Blessing

From my birth and through my youth
I was blessed to see a world full of the changes of God

I have seen those I loved called home to Glory
And others to God's ministry

I have seen and lived in a land and time of
Great oppression and depression
Yet, I have never been forsaken by God

I have watched marches of freedom
Seen fights for equality
Lived through times of war
Nothing is able to detour my service to the Lord

I have raised children, who grow tall and strong
Watched them achieve greatness
But the greatest of all, was when they chose Jesus
And allowed him to live in their hearts
And serving him faithfully

As a century turned in my life's path
I have been blessed to see
The seeds of my mother and father
My children and grandchildren
And all the new changes that God has given us

With a century of memories, thoughts and great blessings
I must give account of my greatest gift in my life
I received is seeing God in my family and having him
Rest deep in my heart.

Water and the Rock

It amazes you that I say I love you
I show you the passion, the love the sincerity
Yet I could walk away from you
You fail to understand I am like the water,
Nothing stands in its way, even a barrier can
Only hinder it for a short time
I love you with each morsel of my heart,
Yet you are not ready to enjoy or accept me,
What I desire to share with you
You are like a rock, stuck in the middle of the rivers
Bed, allowing the water to flow past you
Yet, caress you, sooth you, bring you comfort,
Yet you are not strong enough to notice
That the water is wearing you down
As you continue to let it flow past you
She takes part of your essences from you
Just like age can enhance wine, water can
Stripe you of your strength, your structure.
For you become partial chunks of Sand along
The rivers floor to one day
Just as that woman who loved you
Is no more for you failed to notice
Her, taking you up stream, until you chose to let go

A Better place called Home

Today I laid my eyes to rest
I know it is best...
For with my father is where
I long to be

Rejoice with me I say
For I am in a better place

Here is praises and love
No one is suffering
We are all on one accord

So please don't be sad for me
Just know my love for you is great
But my love for my heavenly father
Is even greater

I look to see you here
Rejoicing in the Lord

God was ready to bring me home
So rejoice in his decision
Give him praises instead of tears
I praise God ...
For I finally made it here
The place I call
Home

Your Touch

It has been your touch that I have
craved for since I first met love

It has been your touch that I desired
to sooth my aches my pains

It is your touch I crave, desire, lust for when it rains

It is your touch that moves my mind
through time and space,

It is your touch that makes me relax and forget the stress

It is your touch that makes the wrongs disappear

It is your touch that removes any of my fears

See your touch has been the one that makes feel secure

It has been your touch that reminds me that there is love

It is your touch that shows love without the lust,

It is your touch that means the world to me

It is your touch and yours alone that makes my heart fill joy

Your touch changed my negative world to positive

It was your touch, as simple as it is that
restored my hope in love.

God knows how I love to feel your touch.

Shelter

When you are in the mist of your
storm let me be your shelter
I may not be able to change the
situation or the circumstances
Yet I can shield you from some of the weather
Let me kneel down next to you and
join you in prayer as you seek guidance
and understanding from God
And while you are yet being still
and preparing to move forward
let me stand next to you slightly at your side
holding your back so that you never fall
softly whispering in your ear strength and reassurance
reminding you of your inner power
reminding you that you are a warrior that
has endured many wars in your life
Mental, physical and definitely spiritual
wars, yet you have always prevailed
remember my love the driving force within you
the one that refuses to surrender let alone die
know that as you keep your eyes on God
you will see the sun beneath the clouds
for the storm must soon pass, while
you wait for a lighter rain,
I want you to know that I am here
As your Shelter from the storm

Reassuring Rain

The rain falls from the sky and seems to
cleanse the sorrow in my heart
Not from heart break, but from concern
for those who are close to me

The touch of each drop on my face,
replaces any tear I have yet to shed
As I think God for each of them are still living and not dead

The rain it seems to sooth me and makes me relax
and think of God's most precious gift to us all, his
son, and how his blood like the rain cleansed all our
sin, and even the stripes he took is able to heal.

The rain became a reminder that as it falls from the
sky, the drops seem endless just as the love God has
for each of us. I can't complain only walk up right and
unashamed for God has delivered us once again.

Yet, as it Rains from the sky, I think of it as a sign,
to remind me of Gods cleansing and healing ability,
it is gentle, it is calm it is always reoccurring.

So as the rain continues to fall, I rest my eyes and tired
body, with reassurance that the prayers I have prayed will
not go unanswered as we cross over to another day.

Forever My Love

To my family and friends with love,

I love each of you more than you can imagine. For those of you who embraced this journey to this very moment, I am forever grateful. I thank God for each word of life you spoke into my life; the word of God gave me such courage to go on especially on the days I really wanted to give up.

To my precious daughter and granddaughter you are truly an extension of God's love that he blessed your Father/Grandfather and I to share. Each moment I held you inspired me to be the best example of a mother I could be. I strived to be a woman that you would want to emulate, as I emulated the love God has shown me. My prayer was to cherish more moments with you than my doctors said I could. God gave those moments to me. Your laughter and the sparkle in your eyes were an energy source to my fading strength. You are a joy that I was blessed to treasure to this moment in time.

Let your memories of me be the joyful ones not the sorrow, think of the tender talks, the shopping sprees and most of all the dreams you shared with me. Live them out, be all that God has destined you to be.

To my love, my strength and my man of God, we didn't start out the way we ended, and that is a blessing for the ending is still yet to be written. As you look at our photo, you know that one favorite one, where we hold each other close, and I have your back and you are my protection. I want you to remember the last 24 years, we have grown together, and matured together, raised our child together. We learned to love, forgive and forget together. I smiled each time I heard your voice, your love it subdued the fear of what was not seen, your touch reminded me that life was so much more and with you my love, we explored many valleys, mountains and distant shores. I rested assured that my heart was yours and yours was mine.

I closed my eyes and exhaled when you spoke the word of God over my life, it was such a comfort and a peace, it was the anchor of my faith. I tried to hold on to every moment I could, but this was the time to let God heal me according to his holy plan. I am whole because I have loved and the Love that God blessed me with by loving each of you.

I am whole because my faith made me whole just like the bible said; God has given me a new body that cannot ever be destroyed, just as the love I was able to receive and also give, it will live in each of you for the rest of this life's journey.

Forever my love,

My Future Awaits Me

My future awaits me and I look out on the
horizon of this thing called Life.
My future and destiny is up to Me, How
far I go How High I rise....
The key to my success is to keep in mind..... God is....
My Source... My Keeper....my Sustainer....My Promoter...
I look at the future that awaits me and I must understand
I will have to trust and work with my fellow man, yet
My destiny is not attached to their decisions on life,
It is My future that awaits...It is my choices that
will carve out the shape of its success
For I know, I have learned, I have obtained and
I can... do all things, as long as I realize,
Even though my future awaits,
I must be wise, I must seek God, and He
is my one and only true Guide.
The Director of my path and in Him, my future
that awaits is one that is truly Blessed.

Old Friend Suicide

Lonely bullet in my chamber I found
Loaded and around I go... Russian
roulette the new game I found

Old friend suicide, how have you been?
Oh yes I am on this disparate street again
Once more I have closed the door and spin the chamber
Click..........

Wow!, I am still here!
What a way to deal with fear

Bye for now suicide my friend
I am sure we shall cross paths again
But, for now reality is set in
A new day for me I must go get

So long old deceitful friend,
Until our paths shall meet again!
Today I live

Even Though......

I often crave your affection
Only to be greeted by your rejection
I often long for your attention
Only to receive your neglection
I desire your romance
Only to receive a blank trance

Yet it is I who is to blame,
For I stayed around
and I played these shallow games

Now, I am the one who experiences pain,
I have suffered through your shame
Yet, alone I am even though ......
I have your name

You Never Knew

How will you feel when you realize that I truly love you
More than anyone else ever could
I wonder how you would feel if me and
my love where no longer here

What would it do for you to know
That for me to love you was all I knew
The pain of that loss is costly too

How will you feel when you realize
How you treated me was so wrong
All I ever wanted or needed was an honest love

How do you feel not that you found this thought
And I am no longer here, but in the ground

Yet, you never knew
I was slowly dying,
hide every now and then by my crying
All for loving to deeply

I thank my God, I am finally able to sleep
Yet you never knew,
That you never knew me!

Was it Worth the Price…?

Did you feel it was worth my hurt, my pain?
The look of shame I received all because of you I believed…
How could you love me you say?
And in the streets you desire to play…
What we had we shared no more…
What was it all for?

Was it truly worth the price it cost?
Was it worth all you lost?
A life of misery, life of loneliness, and event of death….

No more love no more smiles
All that is left is an injured child!

All because you chose to be wild
Was it truly worth the price you paid?
Was it worth it?

Burning Flame

Sometimes I feel as though my life is a
candle with a burning flame
The flame is my passion of which I was always known
Whether for poetry, art or love
Just as time passes and the wax melts
The pain I have endured changed the essence of my being
The flame longing to be the warmth of someone's heart
The beauty and heart of their desire
Destined to be only a flame......
extinguished by the brutal force of wind.

Shades of Black and Gray

Have you ever thought of Life in shades of black and gray?
To see everything the same yet
something different in each one
Not seeing people as different races,
rather seeing them as the loving humans they are
People, who posses beauty in many different ways
Have you tried to imagine being blind?
Always seeing everything the same,
only in shades of black and gray

My Spiritual Fulfillment

Like a whirlwind into my life you came
Neither of us were looking for what God chose to bring
An array of emotions, sense of fulfillment
A knowledge of completion

I feel, no I honestly know that my soul mate does exist
For he came to me out of the mist of my foes

So easily accepted, a lifetime untold
How emotions arose a declaration , no separation
For what God has joined

Operation in the spirit of truth
always on one accord
Funny that all you desire and all you choose to give
I am and I have to offer too

Wisdom I am, Knowledge you are
and together we shall have a beautiful thing
Professions of what God has proclaimed
My destiny had come and my new life has begun

I Am But a Man

Remember I am but a man
It was not I who took 39 lashes of a whip
Nor I who had 3 nails and a crown of thorns

Remember I am but a man....
Not making excuses but at times I will fail
For I am not perfect,
Not me.... only God!

Remember I am but a man...
When I give in to my bodily desires, the lust of my mind
The things I find hard to resist

know that I am but a man...
seeking the perfect will of God

I am not God!
Only a man made in his image
So please, don't criticize
I ask that you pray instead
For I am but a man

Where Would You Be?

I have often spoke about forgiveness , love and devotion
How can I forgive when all I had received
was pain, malice and envy?
Because In my mind God once posed
these questions to me :

Tell me my child, where would you be
If I could no longer forgive you?

Where would you be....
If I harden my heart for the rest of eternity?

Where would you be.....
If I chose no more mercy, no more
grace and no more salvation?

Tell me my child where would you be....
If you walked not in my image, where would you be?

My heart ached as I weep and feel to my knees
Thanking God for all he does every moment for me
So now you know, why I am where I am
Because I was once posed the bone
chilling question from God
Where would you be?

To End You and I

The pain at times is so unbearable
We left each other as friends
Yet you ran to another
I hurt so deeply because I loved you so freely,
Unconditionally
Yet, I am left alone and you moved
on with happiness and bliss

Even though it was rough loving you
I miss that which I cherished
I sleep alone, you in her arms
I watch my son, yours too he is
Yet, through all of this, I know he is solely mine
For you have moved forward and left he and I behind

The choice to leave it was all mine, I had to stop the pain
I could no longer live this lie,
Divorce we have and freedom is yours
You have another, I pray it works this time
All I pray is that you will be the father to our son
For I could not be the one,
You and I did what was best for all,
We let it all go
So Peace to you
Love me

What I Left Behind

A lifetime I have given only to be
stripped by deceit and infidelity
I loved so strongly and deeply but I choose to let you go
I know it is best, you have so much locked inside
That you could never rest
At one point , I thought we would last
I was so wrong
You did not want what I cherished
You dishonored our marriage

To see you with another hurts worst
than any pain I ever endured
Yet, you have peace, with me it will end the same
I beg, I plead that you will seek God,
to redeem what you have lost within yourself
No one on earth can give that which you seek,
Only God
He gave me the strength to go on without you
and see you with your lover and truly smile
For what you lost was far greater
Than that which I left behind

Now That You Know

I have a few questions I long to ask, if I may
Tell me my dear, how do you see me now?
Now that you are truly aware of the truth of my past
The hurt, the pain, love lost and strengths I have gained
How do you view me?
Now that you know
When you see the sparkle in my eyes
What do you feel?
When all I have overcome was
deeply and honestly revealed with
the passion and the pain of those moments
What is the thoughts that went through your mind?
Just how do you see me now?
Now that you truly know,
Just who I am

Printed in the United States
By Bookmasters